B.C.—
The Birthday Cat

B.C.—
The Birthday Cat

Denise Hammerberg

To order additional copies of this book, contact:
Xlibris Corporation
1-888-795-4274
www.Xlibris.com
Orders@Xlibris.com
40897

Contents

Foreword 9

B.C. the Cat— A Poem 12

Chapter 1— The Birthday Cat is Delivered 15

Chapter 2— The Cat Who Acts Like a Dog 21

Chapter 3— The Heat is On! 27

Chapter 4— Ambush Cat 33

Chapter 5— The Office Shredder 37

Chapter 6— Birthday Cat Leaves Presents 43

Chapter 7— The Great Hunter 49

Chapter 8— Alarm Clock Cat 55

Chapter 9— Mama's Good Girl 61

Chapter 10— Trapped!! 65

Chapter 11— Laundry Cat 71

Chapter 12— Chatty Catty 75

Chapter 13— The Unfortunate Sewing Machine Accident 81

Chapter 14— I Want My Yogurt! 87

Chapter 15— Therapist in a Fur Coat 91

Chapter 16— Still, Mama's Good Girl 97

A Wish for our Readers 101

Afterword— by Dolly Arksey 103

DEDICATION

This book is dedicated to my daughter, Lindsay, and my husband, Ken, without whom there never would have been a Birthday Cat story. Thanks for your love, being yourselves, and having enough flexibility to welcome B.C., this little delight of my life, into our family.

Love,
Denise

Foreword

The inspiration for the *B.C., The Birthday Cat* book was sparked during a conversation I was having with the author, my daughter Denise Hammerberg. She and I had just seen our first co-authored book published, titled *The Garden of Being*, a daughter-mother memoir of a family dealing with cancer. While we were still basking in the glow of accomplishment, we were both eager to tackle new projects. I had recently read *Marley & Me*, by John Grogan, a story about a man and his dog which made the national best seller list, and suggested to Denise that she should write a book for cat lovers about her and the never-ending adventures of her faithful, funny, feline friend 'for keeps', B.C.

A year earlier, at age forty-four, Denise had heard the doctor's words, "You have cancer. It's stage IV". The shock of this message was absolutely earth shaking considering she never missed an annual physical examination in the previous ten years, including dreaded mammograms. But she, herself, had discovered an almond-size lump on her neck some months after her last annual physical check up. A biopsy determined the lump to be a malignant tumor resulting from metastatic breast cancer. We learned from reading medical resource material that stage IV cancer meant life expectancy was less than five years, usually much less; but we did not speak aloud about the depressing statistics, hoping that positive action and advances in treatment protocols would help her beat the odds. Most of all, we prayed for a miracle. Chemotherapy started immediately; and with no realistic plans for Denise to return to her management work in the automotive supply field, she turned to writing as a creative pursuit. During six months of chemotherapy, she worked diligently on her treatment and a healthy, healing foods regimen. She and all our family were dedicated to positive thinking. In her naturally feisty and spirited way, during her "good days", she poured herself into creative projects—writing, cooking, working in the flower and vegetable gardens, holiday gift planning and preparation, contacting friends and home decorating projects.

When Denise had completed the initial six months of chemo treatment, our family felt we were blessed with a true miracle when her X-rays and scans did not detect any tumor activity. It was a time of guarded optimism and hope, but most of all, it was a time for living and loving.

The following months of celebration and freedom from chemo treatments for Denise and keeping a positive mindset fed her creativity and joy. It was during this time she began to write *B.C., The Birthday Cat.*

Eight months later, tests showed the cancer had resurfaced. The oncology physician told her bluntly that it was an aggressive type of cancer in the lungs. Denise asked the oncologist face-to-face for the facts about her prognosis, and the doctor's words were tactfully ambiguous, "Everyone has to die sometime, we just don't know when that will be or how. Isn't that true?" These words were mind numbing and made my heart nearly stop. Denise and I stood for several moments looking at the doctor as if our bodies and thoughts were frozen in time. Neither of us cried audibly, but our eyes were filling with tears. At least, I thought, the doctor's words did not deny the hope that Denise would have more than a little time to share with her loved ones on this earth. More chemotherapy was the only option the doctor could offer. I was personally grateful that the doctor had not said 'six to seven months' or some specific number that would begin a countdown of calendar days. This way, we could keep a tight hold on hope for better news than we just heard. Hope is like a life line, keeping us connected to a safe place in our heart.

Denise finished the *B.C., The Birthday Cat* book manuscript shortly before her death at age forty-six. She would be very proud to see her book in print; but as I saw first-hand, she experienced much joy in the process of writing the book. I think she was anxious to share her and B.C.'s personal story with others to show how a small creature such as a cat, so different from us and yet providing such mysterious compatibility, can bring immeasurable love and happiness into our human life during good times and hard times.

I am attempting to fill the cavernous hole in my heart caused by the loss of my daughter by filling it with memories of happy times. Rereading the stories about her favorite memories of B.C., help me to remember each and every time Denise had told me by phone or in person about her cat's comical adventures. I can still hear her voice saying "Guess what B.C. did today?" in a teasing tone of voice and almost see the twinkle in her eyes when she talked about B.C.'s latest predicament.

By example, Denise taught me these important things during her illness which I treasure as gifts of love from her 1) to be brave in the face of death and 2) to show and tell the people you care about that you love them at every opportunity. She was and she did.

*   *   *

Foreword by Dolly Arksey

B.C. THE CAT by Denise Hammerberg

She showed up one sunny summer day,
Tossed in the road in a haphazard way.

In sleeping all day and out hunting all night,
Roaming through weeds leaves her fur an awful fright!

Her diet includes yogurt in the morning,
Not getting it in time prompts a ferocious "warning".

One thing you can count on, she'll never be tardy,
When someone in the neighborhood is having a party.

Hiding behind plants, fences and rocks,
Her ambushing skills scare you right out of your socks.

She always tries to help when there's laundry to fold,
Off she'll run with a sock, not taking it where she's told.

Knows what she wants and won't give up 'til it's gotten . . .
Some people might say she's spoiled rotten.

B.C. the cat sure does give our life a boost,
Still it's easy to see that it's she who rules the roost.

Chapter 1

—The Birthday Cat is Delivered

It has to be assumed that you purchased this book, at least in part, because you were smitten by the sweet little face of the beautiful cat on the cover of this book.

Meet B.C.

At the time of this writing, B.C., the beauty that she is, is three, almost four, years old, ever so slightly over seven pounds and lives a comfortable, fairly routine existence in Lapeer, Michigan. She has, however, like many of us; taken a few detours on this journey we call life.

What follows is her story, not as chronology but rather each chapter as a short story showing one of her many 'lives' or personalities. Like some people, B.C. and I imagine most animals have different personalities that emerge for different times or conditions in their lives.

She showed up on a beautiful, sunny summer day. We had just had a family birthday party for our daughter, Lindsay. As Lindsay and I relaxed in her bedroom discussing the events of the day, and gazing out the window, we noticed a boy walking down our suburban street swinging something in his hand. Whatever was inside the bundle the boy was carrying seemed to be moving; but, I, not wearing my glasses, couldn't quite make out what he was holding. As we peered out the window, suddenly he flipped open what turned out to be a blanket and out popped the scrawniest kitten I had ever seen. She shot away from the boy and his blanket like a small, furry rocket and headed toward our house. As she made her way up our driveway, the two of us ran out of the bedroom and onto our front porch. We were somewhat surprised at how trusting this little orphan appeared, boldly walking right up our driveway, responding to our "oh's and ah's' and tender calls of 'kitty, kitty, kitty'.

She was, without a doubt, the most pitiful little cat I had ever seen. She was a tangled mess of long, matted orange hair with a tail that appeared larger than the whole rest of her body. Her ears were black with ear mites and fleas. She reminded me of one of those cheap and worn out stuffed animals with very little stuffing, all hair and no meat on her bones. Even in her unkempt condition her fur was softer than the most expensive cashmere sweater I have ever touched. And despite the lack of attention she had obviously been subjected to, she came right to us; rubbing against our ankles. She seemed to crave the tender touch of our hands. Like mother lions we held her, fed her what we had in the kitchen (milk and crab meat, quite a gourmet meal for a stray!) and 'cooed' over her delicate features and sweet, tender nature.

But it was getting late and we were getting sleepy. Lindsay and I returned to the house and went about our nightly routine of getting ready for bed. Soon afterward we heard my husband, Ken, in the garage gruffly scolding, "Go on, Git!"; and we scurried out to the garage. He looked at us and said, "I keep shooing this cat out of the garage, but it keeps coming back". Sheepishly, I had to admit that I had fed her; and, even though I knew neither of us were interested in the drawbacks and inconvenience of having a pet, I begged him to let her stay. "Look at how skinny she is! Look at that sweet little face". I think he knew it was useless to fight my maternal urges and he relented to at least let her stay for a night or two. Who knew, maybe she would mysteriously leave as quickly as she showed up.

A few hours later our neighbor, Brian Jones, came over to visit and met our new house guest. Helpful, as always, his wife, Julie, still talks of her surprise when he went home and was looking for kitty litter. Kitty litter? Brian? The man who had never stooped to scoop their cat's litter box, EVER???

Later in the evening, Julie fell in love with the tiny, emaciated kitten, too. She went home and, in typical neighborly fashion, brought back cat treats and a brush which she used for hours to work through this kitten's tangled and matted fur. As we fawned over her and laughed about her showing up at Lindsay's birthday party, we decided that she was "The Birthday Cat" and we would call her B.C. for short.

It didn't dawn on me until the next day that B.C. had shown up *exactly* 17 years to the day from when I had brought my baby girl Lindsay home from the hospital to this very house. While I pondered just what might come into my life 17 years from now; it was then that it struck me that there was no way I could give up this new arrival. Call it fate, call it the stars lining up, or call it whatever you want. I knew in my heart of hearts that, showing up on this day, she belonged to us and nothing would ever change that.

B.C. had been delivered to us from a force greater than ourselves and we were destined to be together.

Cat Chat

- *According to a Gallup poll, most American pet owners obtain their cats by adopting strays.*

- *More than 35,000 kittens are born in the U.S. each year. Spay or neuter your cat.*

- *The average lifespan of an outdoor-only cat is three years. An indoor-only cat can live 16 years or longer*

- *The typical male housecat will weigh between seven and nine pounds, slightly less for female housecats*

Chapter 2

—The Cat Who Acts Like a Dog

B.C. spent the first six months with us relegated to our garage for precautionary measures. Every day before work I would fill her dish with food, change her water and watch her to be sure she stayed put in the garage while I closed the garage door when I went to work. And there she would be when I returned, bright-eyed and happy to see me. She would run up to the car 'talking' to me the whole time; as if to tell me, "I've been here *all* day waiting to play!"

B.C. became the socialite of the neighborhood and quickly took over the unfenced wide-open backyard formed by our house and our five surrounding neighbors. This became her territory which she guarded like a fierce miniature lioness. There were a couple of dogs and a few other inside cats (that she taunted unmercifully that first year) but no one to challenge her status as the dominant cat in her territory.

The neighbors all loved her. Nathan Jones, our neighbors' young son, put it sweetly when he petted her silky fur and said, "She's so soft, she makes me smile!"

I would have been a little peeved if my neighbor's cat walked on my car, but Pete Folco, our neighbor from the top of the hill, diplomatically said he was happy to see tiny, muddy paw prints as signs she was there stalking the area for mice.

I started bragging to everyone she was 'more than a cat'. B.C. was like a dog.

- Just like a dog she followed us wherever we roamed in the neighborhood
- Just like a dog she would come when you called her
- Just like a dog she would sleep at the foot of our bed at night

- Just like a dog she could sense when you were upset and would purr, lick your hand with her delicate, tiny tongue and peer into your face as if to say, "It's ok, I love you."

If we all met to have a bonfire in the backyard, B.C. would invariably be there, jumping after lightning bugs or climbing high in trees to show off her acrobatic skills. Sometimes you didn't even know she was there, but as we would walk home on late evenings, she would shoot across the yard just ahead of us, eager to get home, too.

Cat Chat

- *Sociable cats will follow you from room to room to monitor your activities throughout the day.*

- *The nose pad of a cat is ridged in a pattern that is unique, just like the fingerprint of a human.*

- *A cat will almost never "meow" at another cat. This sound is reserved for humans.*

- *Ailurophobia is the fear of cats. Julius Caesar, Henry II, Charles XI and Napoleon were said to have suffered from this ailment. People with this phobia may experience extreme anxiety and feel that they may faint.*

- *Ailurophilia is the love of cats. If you bought this book, you probably have this condition.*

Chapter 3

—The Heat is On!

After the first few days, when Ken and I agreed that B.C. would be a permanent part of our family, I took her to the vet. We got started with the first shot required for immunization and flea medicine which the doctor told me would cure her ear mites, too. It appeared that she was healthy and old enough to get spayed despite her tiny size, so I scheduled that procedure to coincide with the next shot which was required in three weeks. Feeling pretty smug about my fine scheduling skills which would limit the number of times my 'baby' would have to travel in the car, we headed home.

I should take this time to explain just how exciting the ride to the vet was, especially for any of you who don't have a cat. My sweet natured, loveable kitten became a wild tiger in the cage as soon as the car started moving. B.C. 'roared' at the top of her lungs and frantically stretched her front legs out of any hole large enough to get them through and reached out to *ANYTHING* she thought might help get her out of the cage. I spent the 15 minute ride there and back trying to comfort her as I drove, but nothing would settle her down. I talked to her. I sang to her. I 'cooed' to her. Nothing made her stop until we returned home. So as I said, I was patting myself on the back for combining two appointments into one because, of course, her comfort was foremost from this point on.

Life went along on a regular routine for a few days after that. For awhile, that is. Then suddenly my sweet, loveable kitten was acting berserk! I had never had cats that were not spayed at a very young age; so I had never witnessed the complete chaos of a female cat being '*in heat*'. I thought she had been shot, bitten by a snake or something even worse. Every time I would try to get near her, she would run away. She would then proceed to screech at the top of her lungs. What was going on? Panic set in. She was after all, my baby. My sweet little cat that acted like a dog sometimes, and, now she had become nearly demonic!

A friend suggested that maybe she was *in heat* (period of time that female cats are receptive to impregnation by a male cat). I called the after-hours animal clinic. Did the symptoms sound like she was *in heat*? *Yes.* She was scheduled for spaying in ten days. Would there be an extra cost if she was pregnant? *Yes.* Would she stay *in heat* for these ten days? Possibly.

Minimizing her car trips would be the goal due to B.C.'s aversion to cages and 'car sickness' syndrome. I took her to the vet the next day for spaying and another exciting car ride. I learned the true meaning of why the term 'caged animal' means "Do Not Touch!"

Cat Chat

- *Female cats are "polyestrous" which means they many have many heat periods over the course of a year. A heat period lasts about four to seven days if the female is bred; if she is not, the heat period lasts longer and recurs at regular intervals.*

- *Calico cats are almost always female. Long haired orange tabby type cats are almost always male. (not B.C, who was an exception, as our friendly veterinarian pointed out during one visit).*

- *A single pair of cats and their kittens can produce as many as 420,000 kittens in just 7 years! A cat's gestation period is 61-65 days.*

Chapter 4

—Ambush Cat

Everyone in our 'community' yard area was ambushed by B.C. at least once; and, so, she also became 'Ambush Cat'.

When she was a tiny kitten she would hide under beds and behind doors, waiting for that perfect time to jump out, grab your ankles ever so gently with her front paws and then scurry for cover. She brought laughter and playfulness to our lives.

Tall ornamental grass grew in the backyard and by mid-summer it frequently 'grew' a large, orange tail. For hours she would wait in the tall grass clumps for anyone or anything to pass by so she could jump out and play the 'Gotcha!' game by grasping softly at your ankles. People, to her, were mere play things, like birds, mice or grasshoppers, just bigger.

B.C. loved gardening. Her dog-like qualities are never more visible than when we are working in the yard. She follows us to whatever corner of the yard we are working in, running gleefully around to 'investigate' what is happening in the yard; always waiting for the perfect time to ambush you from behind one plant or another. When she tires of our current activity, she sits for hours in the shade watching us, staying cool, but ever ready to go on to the next project.

I brought home a new plant one day. CATNIP. She LOVED it and went into a swoon, rolling over and over against the intoxicating leafy plant. By the end of the first week the plant was nothing but a nub of a stalk with *a few* greenish strands lying limp on the ground. I read somewhere that not every cat gets 'high' from catnip and that whether or not a cat responds to it depends upon a recessive gene: No gene, No joy. No problem—she's got it!

Sometimes B.C. will be gardening with you and you won't even know it, as our neighbor, Julie Jones, found out one day when B.C. sent her screaming and running from a 'surprise ambush' as she was weeding the corn in her garden. Julie had been slightly shocked, but that's all.

To B.C., it seems, we all were playmates for her 'Gotcha!' game.

Cat Chat

- *A feline in a hurry can sprint at about thirty-one miles per hour.*

- *Warning! Watch for these signs that may indicate a cat is in the attack or defensive mode and may bite:*

  1) cat's body will tense and spine may curve upward

  2) ears will likely tuck back against head

  3) pupils may dilate

  4) a tail flicking side to side.

  Do not approach or touch a cat exhibiting these signs!

- *Cats have 30 vertebrae. Humans have 25.*

- *A group of kittens is called a kindle. A group of cats is called a clowder.*

Chapter 5

—The Office Shredder

I have never thought of cats as particularly destructive. Our previous kittens had always come in pairs (for companionship) and had been de-clawed early on because they were inside cats. Being an outside hunter and assigned to mouse patrol was part of B.C.'s job now, so I couldn't have her de-clawed. This led to the discovery of one of her less charming abilities.

Shredding.

She will shred newspapers. She will shred rolls of paper towel. She will shred toilet paper, magazines, and, yes, even bills. It's too bad that isn't an acceptable way to 'handle' them!

Every so often I would head into the bathroom to find the toilet paper not only unrolled in a large, messy pile, but with large chunks gouged right out of the whole roll. You can't forget the incident for a few days because you are still using toilet paper with holes in it. Although I never figured out what made her mad enough to tear apart the toilet paper, we must have ultimately become trained to avoid offending her because she has not done it in quite awhile. She still does, however, like to shred paper when given an opportunity. In fact, ironically, today she had a confrontation with the printer and shredded this particular draft page in defiance as if to say "Yea, I'm the shredder, what's it to ya?"

My husband may very well be the only Daddy to have received a homemade (with help from mommy me) Valentine's Day card from their cat. The message read:

Things I Do to Get Your Attention

- *Make you mad by shredding paper towels (written on a shredded paper towel to prove it)*
- *Help wrap presents*
  (a note on birthday wrapping paper with claw marks)
- *Keep your lap warm*
- *Love you a lot*

Love, B.C.

As B.C. has gotten older her curiosity about noises has lead her to shred my printed pages as they hop scotch out of my home office printer. She will also run from any corner of our home to sit and watch with rapt attention whenever the *real* shredder goes into motion, buzzing like a beehive as it goes through its cycle.

I took this as a sign that she was maturing and taking an interest in business. Soon, she had another nickname, Office Cat.

As far as assistants go, however, I would fire her in a New York minute. She is as unhelpful and distracting as an ineffective one. Too much fluff, a lot of bad habits and no help with productivity.

Lucky for her, except for mouse patrol duties, she isn't required to earn her keep in any other way than loving us and making us laugh. She works overtime at that!

Cat Chat

- *I read somewhere that dogs have owners and cats have servants. It sure has worked that way in our household!*

- *To deter a cat from bad habits such as scratching furniture, use the "pennies in a can" trick. When you catch cat in the act, shake the can. It usually works as the noise frightens them, but is painless.*

- *Provide scratching posts or carpeted play 'stations' for cast to sharpen and groom their claws. Praise cats when they use these.*

- *Keep a small mister/spray bottle filled with plain water handy. Give cat a small squirt only when you catch them in the act performing a 'bad' habit. Any other time they will just think you are nuts or a big meany!*

- *There are several commercial products on the market to use in controlling unacceptable cat behaviors. Check with your Vet or local pet store.*

- The 'kneading' activity of cats upon a soft surface or a human body is an inborn instinct which starts at birth and stimulates milk production of the mother cat when the kitten is nursing. A cat will continue to do this throughout its life, as it is good exercise for its paws and legs.

- A cat's claws are a masterpiece of engineering and are its chief weapon of defense and self-preservation. A de-clawed cat is extremely vulnerable to any predator. De-clawing is painful, major surgery and may create serious physical ailments or biting habits.

- Alternatives to de-clawing a cat are 1) finding a new home for the cat where it has room to roam and a cat-friendly environment or 2) clip nails regularly or apply nail caps such as SoftPaws, which are plastic tips glued on the cat's own claws. An application should last six weeks. These alternatives are a much kinder solution that de-clawing which does nothing to benefit the cat, but creates great suffering.

Chapter 6

—Birthday Cat Leaves Presents

B.C. had been with us for awhile, roaming the neighborhood at her leisure, when we found out about a habit she had that made her less than popular with our next door neighbors, the Joneses. You see, her litter boxes in our basement were seldom used; probably only at times she was shut in and we weren't home to let her out. I always assumed she had found somewhere outside (hopefully not my flower beds or garden) and the arrangement worked well.

Unfortunately, shortly after the spring thaw, our neighbors witnessed B.C., in the act of using their kids' sandbox for her personal super-sized litter box. This might have been bad enough; but it came to be common knowledge that their dog, Casey, a just-under-100-pound Labrador Retriever, would act as a canine Pooper Scooper and eat the unwrapped 'presents'. *YUCK.* The worst part of this story was once when Julie, the mom and a registered nurse, came home from work one evening at midnight and received a big, sandy, smelly kiss from her dog Casey. She was not very happy when she heard the story from her kids about the 'snacks' Casey had been seen eating earlier!

Lauren, the Jones' middle child, asked me to "Please have a talk with B.C. and ask her NOT to do that anymore". I guess this is a testament to how un-cat like B.C. really is. Lauren thought B.C. would really understand if I gave the mischievous cat a 'good talking' to!

A 'present' of another kind was discovered one evening as my husband, Ken, and I snuggled with B.C. on the couch. One of us saw something blue hanging around B.C.'s tail. Upon further investigation it was discovered that it was a strand of skinny blue curling ribbon, the kind you use for wrapping gifts, and it wasn't just hanging *on* her, it was hanging *from* inside her, tape dispenser style! B.C. must have been chewing on ribbon and ended up swallowing a piece that (based on what we could see) was over six inches long. She balked when we tried to gently tug and pull it out, so we let her go and decided to let nature take its course. I'm not sure where the blue ribbon ended up and I did not waste time looking for it, but the next day, B.C. was fine. I haven't, however, been able to wrap a gift with curling ribbon since without feeling a tiny bit nauseous and making sure I don't leave any ribbon around for the cat to chew on!

These type of presents from B.C. can be labeled "Final Sale Items—Non-returnable".

Cat Chat

- *Cats take personal hygiene very seriously. Some cats will not urinate if their litter box is in a noisy area. Like humans, felines like privacy and quiet in their bathrooms. A good thing about cats is that they never complain about people leaving the toilet seat up!*

- *Clean litter container daily to control odor and also to protect your cat and yourself from bacterial infections.*

Chapter 7

—The Great Hunter

She was the great hunter of the neighborhood. B.C. would bring home trophies of the hunt and all the neighbors would tell stories of seeing her 'spear' a mole in the yard or trap a frog in their window wells. Mice were the most frequent captures; but the most unusual 'catch' came when she ran into the garage with a 12-inch long white snake. It was wriggling for dear life. For her this was the ultimate toy; easy to catch and robust enough to withstand a good deal of rough housing, unlike grasshoppers and mice which tired out and gave up the fight much too quickly for her!

Sometimes it occurs to me that the sweet little face that rubs up to mine and the soft little paws that touch my face to wake me up when she wants out are also used to kill; and, yes, even eat the least appetizing morsels found outside. Luckily, this does not happen often. It is simply the wild basic instinct of all felines, large and small.

More often I just revel in that sweet face, luminescent gold eyes and soft touch, accepting her for all that she is and for being my funny, furry friend.

We had a scare due to her 'lifestyle' choice of hunting one April day. My husband, Ken, had found the wings to a bird a few days early and after that B.C. came running into the house with eyes dilated, looking to us like she was trying to run away from herself; only stopping periodically to bite herself under her front legs. What was wrong with my baby? Did she eat something poisonous? I called the vet immediately. She was due for a wormer. Could that possible be the cause of her behavior? The vet gave us the medicine on a Friday afternoon and told us to monitor her to see that she didn't have an obstruction. In layman's terms they said we should make sure she was going to the bathroom with 'results'. I do not think they understood what a challenge this would be for us since she is used to coming and going on her own time table. Happily, by Saturday afternoon she was back to her old self. I do not think we will ever know if it was the worm medicine that helped her or if she just worked whatever was ailing her out of her system through natural processes. But, what a relief to have our happy little hunter back to normal!

Yes, her trophies sometimes surprised or grossed you out, but I've come to learn what pride looks like when your cat brings you a catch like a luckless mouse swinging from her jaws. Her head and tail high, she prances up to you like a Shetland pony. The Great Hunter she is!

Cat Chat

- Cats are not vegetarians and should never be put on a vegetarian diet. Cats are flesh eaters and need to eat meat.

- According to a pet food industry magazine survey, cat food sales totaled eight billion dollars in 2002, believe it or not.

- Chocolate is toxic to cats. The darker the chocolate, the more dangerous.

- When your cat rubs up against you, marking you with scent from the glands near his whiskers, take it as a compliment—the cat is claiming you as his own.

- Cats are not truly 'nocturnal', but 'crepuscular' which means they are most active at dawn and dusk. Outdoor cats hunt during these times because this is when their prey is usually active.

- Cats cannot see in total darkness although they have good night vision.

- Top U.S. cat breed is reported to be Persian.

- **Cat sayings and myths:**

It's raining cats and dogs. (The cat is supposed to have influence on weather according to northern mythology. Witches assumed the form of a cat which rode on storm winds. Odin, the storm god was attended by a dog and a wolf, both signs of the wind.)

Like something the cat dragged in. (of unkempt appearance)

When the cat's away the mice will play. (When person in charge is absent, people will take advantage of the situation)

Chapter 8

—Alarm Clock Cat

Maybe this chapter should have been named *Terror in the Bedroom* or *Nighttime Nuisance*; either would have been appropriate, but I decided on calling B.C. the *Alarm Clock Cat* because her antics usually do not happen until 4:00 a.m. or painfully early pre-dawn hours.

Many a sound sleep has been interrupted by the soft, gentle touch of her left paw on my face. Could it be that cat's have tendencies, such as humans, to be right or left-handed? Ignoring her urgings does not cause her to go away; it just steps up her insistence. She will try this two or three times despite having to nudge under the covers where I eventually hide for cover. She will not be ignored. If I don't succumb to her 'demands' she will move on to more annoying 'insistences' that I get up and either:

a) let her outside

b) feed her

c) *(or the most frustrating)* chase her around the house in the one-sided fun game of middle of the night 'Tag'.

If I am slightly successful at ignoring the first cheek-tapping tactics at waking me, B.C. moves on to more aggressive antics that will wake up Dad (Ken). The most common of these is pawing on our mirrored closet doors which makes them rattle like a wind-whipped screen door. This is meant to wake us up with more fanfare and audio effects since politely requesting with her soft paws did not produce the desired results. This is not a pretty scenario. My husband, Ken, is much less tolerant of her bad habits and does not see it as cute in any way, shape or form. He will shut her out of the bedroom or start in his own game of "pillow fight" with her. His theory is that if we get up and 'give in' to what he sees as coercion, that she will always do it. And he believes he can get her trained with his 'stand firm' policy. So far this has not worked.

I have tried to explain to B.C., using lots of sweet talk, several times that this activity would not be so bad if it happened after 6:00 a.m. on weekdays and 8:00 a.m. on weekends, but I think her internal cat clock runs on a nocturnal time zone and does not understand what a commotion she causes at such early hours. We have come to identify that, while she wants *what* she wants *when* she wants it, her biggest motivator might be coveted space. Many a morning after we've fought the fight, but lost the battle, and let her outside, she will be at the window waiting to come back in and join me on the bed after my husband gets up to get ready for work—always laying right in the middle of his vacant, but still toasty warm spot!

She operates on B.C. time which has no correlation to kronos time. She just does what she does when she feels like it. Nice way to live, eh? Maybe I should just train myself to rise when she does. I doubt that will happen. For now, I will do my best to hop up and let her out before she disrupts her dad. She is my fuzzy, early morning alarm clock who does not need batteries, electricity or winding.

Cat Chat

- To encourage your cat to sleep through the night: 1) play with cat before bedtime and 2) feed largest meal before bedtime.

- Ignore cat's nighttime behaviors. Like a child, if you respond to the attention-getting antics and they get what they want, the behaviors will continue.

- Do not feed cat first thing in the morning if possible. Cat will wake owner up to ask "Is breakfast ready?"

- Out of every 100 cats approximately 40 are left-pawed, 20 are right-pawed and 40 are ambidextrous.

Chapter 9

—Mama's Good Girl

B.C. has a tender, cuddly side to her personality that can melt the hardest of hearts. She is like a little orange angel complete with a cloud of silky, fuzzy, fur but *only* angelic when she feels like it; and, without a doubt, that part of her personality is *ALL* cat. Everyone comments on her soft hair when they get the privilege of being able to touch her. Her fur is like the softest of cashmere or angora, the delicate down of a newborn chick or the coat of a baby rabbit.

Upon investigating different breeds of cats on the internet, I spotted a photo and believed I found a close relative of B.C. The breed is called Somali and I decided that was the breed she must be, at least in part. The physical characteristics and habits matched up perfectly.

Somalis are active, playful and interactive. They love to have lots of room to roam and lots of personal attention. Other traits are: 1) even temper 2) people-oriented (party animals) 3) clever 4) curious 5) minimal shedding of hair and 6) "Dog-Like" in behaviors (just like I told friends, B.C. is more like a dog than a cat).

Physical characteristics of Somalis which also describe B.C. are: 1) medium size 2) coloration often like a fox (commonly reddish gold with dark brown ticking) 3) brushy tail 4) distinctive "M" pattern on forehead 5) gold eyes (like B.C.) or green and 6) good communicators and companions.

The longer she was with us, the more I started treating her like my baby. The neighbors, especially our neighborhood 'Lawn Enforcement Officer', Dave Oparka, would get a good laugh whenever I would fawn over her with baby talk like "How's Mama's good girl? What's her want? Aww, go say hi to daddy".

Many an evening would result in B.C. sleeping in my lap stretched out like a human baby; head on my arm and her belly snug against mine for warmth and protection. Ken would always laugh and say "She's not comfortable at all, is she"?

Cat Chat

- Just like for a troubled child, we forgive our pets their shortcomings and love them for just being themselves.

- Cats get their sense of security from your voice. Talk to your cats! The more cats are spoken to, the more they will speak to you.

- Cats have about 100 different vocalization sounds that they can use in communicating.

- A cat's tail held high signals they are happy. A twitching tail signals danger; don't mess with this cat! A tail tucked close to the body signals insecurity.

- Cats' eyes—In relation to body size, cats have the largest eyes of any mammal.

Chapter 10

—Trapped!!

One sad day I couldn't find B.C. She failed to come home after her regular 'night out'. I had to go to work, so I was hopeful that she would be back upon my return that evening. No such luck. I was frantic and depressed! I tried to rationalize, telling myself 'easy come, easy go'. But inside, my heart was breaking. She was so little, so cute, so sweet. My constant companion.

I checked out all the previous places she had been 'trapped' before:

- the pantry in the basement where she frequently sneaks in unnoticed only to cry out when someone finally asks 'Where's the cat"? *No cat.*
- I checked the garage; up in the rafters, on the old motorcycle where she would sometimes perch like an easy rider, in the closets (could she have wandered in unnoticed?). *Still no cat.*

That night I was out of bed half a dozen times, hoping she would run up to the back window, touching her face flat against the glass it as if to say "Hey, I'm right here, let me in." But she did not. Off to work I went once again, heart heavy, scolding myself for being such a softy. I mean, really, wasn't she just a cat? My head said yes, my heart said no. When I came home from work on the second day and still no B.C. in sight, I decided it was time to put our neighbors on high alert. Had anyone seen her? Nope. She wasn't in the pool house at the Joneses. She wasn't in Pete and Star Folco's garage. Dave hadn't seen her up taunting his dog, Pooh. "Where, oh, where could my little dog (cat) be? Oh where, oh where had she gone??" My heart was breaking.

On the third day I received a call from the next-door neighbor, Julie Jones. Had B.C. been missing? The way she asked I thought she was just following up from my call yesterday to her husband, Brian, the night before. "Yes", I told her sadly, B.C. had been gone for two nights.

"I think I found her", she told me. Holding my breath I waited for her answer. What did she mean, she 'thought' she had found her??

Just as we finished those sentences, here came B.C., nose flat against our dining room window, looking peeved as could be and meowing with all her might to be let in.

As I let B.C. in the house, with the quickest of 'hellos', she was off to her food bowl, Julie told me the story of how, while watching her daughter, Lauren, get on the bus at noon that day, something caught her eye in their SUV in her driveway. It startled her because there was *something* moving back and forth across the dash of the vehicle. After a few times she realized it was a cat. When Julie opened the SUV door to let the captive cat out, B.C. shot out of the vehicle like a streak of lightning, more than a little miffed and fitting the description of a true "scared cat"!

Once it was calculated when it would have been possible for her to have become locked inside the vehicle, it didn't surprise anyone that she had had to 'relieve' herself during her captivity and left tell-tale signs. Forty-eight hours without bathroom privileges is impossible for anyone, man or beast.

Upon investigation and interrogation it was thought that Nathan, the youngest of the Jones's three children, may have shut B.C. in the car to keep her at their house because he liked her. I think it is more likely that B.C. snuck in while the kids had the doors opened and missed the opportunity to exit before the vehicle had been locked up for the night.

And I would have liked to think this experience taught her not to be climbing into any vehicles again; however, we found this to not be the case when she took up residency in an older van we had parked in the yard ourselves a few months later. Fortunately, this time she had a way in and out—until the motor cover was replaced anyway.

Cat Chat

- *A cat's whiskers, called vibrissae, grow on the cat's face as well as the backs of its forelegs. The whiskers help a cat gauge the space it intends to walk through. By the way, if a cat's whiskers are cut off for any reason, they will grow back. (A fact that came in handy with a previous cat, Georgia, whom suffered this indignity at the hands of my daughter, Lindsay when Linds was only eight years old).*

- *Kittens have 'baby' teeth which are replaced with adult teeth around six months of age.*

- *Cats perspire through their paws.*

- *Cats breath at rate of 20-30 breaths per minute. Normal pulse if 110-140 beats per minute. Body temperature normally is 102 degrees Fahrenheit.*

Chapter 11

—Laundry Cat

There isn't a house chore I like less than folding laundry. It is picky work, quite not in line with my 'do-it-when-you-feel-like-it' procrastinating personality. I came to like it a little more, though, when B.C. took an interest in helping me.

At first it irritated me when she started 'stealing' articles of laundry. I'd run around in circles to catch her, afraid she might damage something. From room to room, just as I'd get to her, she'd dart in a different direction with whatever she had stolen clenched firmly between her teeth, tail and head high and proud. But nothing ever got damaged, maybe lost for a day or two, but never damaged; so I started to lighten up a tad.

She also loved to jump into the laundry basket. Not all the time, only when I emptied it and busied myself folding the clothes that had been in residence there. We would put the basket on its side and roll her slowly across the room which only made her scrunch herself smaller to ensure not falling out. I can tip the whole basket over on top of her to which her only reaction is to blink calmly at me and reach her front paws out through the openings to engage me in a game of 'Gotcha!'. Could she touch me and get back inside without me grabbing her? Could I stick my fingers in the holes and wiggle it around without her making me 'It'? She made doing laundry a little bit more fun. Look, I will never be the Queen of the Laundry, but B.C. puts some smiles and more than a little fun into the job.

Cat Chat

- Cats are in category of the least domesticated of house pets.

- One un-neutered female cat can, within about five years, breed over 20,000 descendents.

- It is estimated that there are 60 million feral (wild) cats living on the streets in the United States.

- The cat is the only domesticated animal not mentioned in the Bible (?)

- The U.S. cat population is estimated at 76,500,000-plus.

Chapter 12

—Chatty Catty

B.C. is a quiet cat. She does not meow a lot. She relies on her paws and body language to tell you that she wants something, but she can be an accomplished conversationalist when she so desires.

Mornings when you wake up or anytime when you let her in from outside you are normally given a quick melodic "rrrrrrrrrrrppp" (I call it 'trilling') as if to say "Hello" or "Hey what's going on?" And, if she feels she is being ignored, you will invariably be given the same type of greeting to ensure you aren't concentrating on anything other than her.

The most memorable time she 'talked' to us happened as my husband, Ken, and I were having a serious conversation about my upcoming cancer treatment; and Ken, in his usual nurturing fashion, told me not to worry, that we were in this together and "united we stand". The serious tension was broken when B.C. immediately entered her own two cents worth of "rrrrrrrrrrrppp" to which Ken replied, "Yes, and you too, little one". There is no doubt, we are a family.

Cat Chat

- Cats get a sense of security from tone and volume of a human voice. Most cats seem to like to be spoken to and will often return 'vocalization'.

- The reason a cat purrs raises more than one theory! Some theories include:

  1. Purring is caused by vibration of 'false' vocal cords when inhaling and exhaling.

  2. Purring is intended to communicate contentment and relaxation.

  3. Rhythmic impulses to the cat's larynx cause purring noises.

  4. Cats purr for other cats as well as for humans.

  5. Unproven, but yet another theory is cats may purr to help generate vibration frequencies in their body to promote healing energies. Maybe this is why some cats purr when they are hurt or sick.

6. Maybe it just feels good, like a person humming a happy tune.

- The phrase, *enough to make a cat laugh*, is said to mean something ridiculous.

- The phrase, *enough to make a cat speak*, is said to mean that strong liquor will loosen one's tongue.

- The phrase, *to let the cat out of the bag*, means to disclose a secret. The story goes that in the 18th century, when piglets were taken to market in a sack called a poke, the con men would put a cat in the sack to pass it off as a pig. If the cat struggled too much, it would have to be let out, exposing the secret.

Chapter 13

—The Unfortunate Sewing Machine Accident

One cold, winter day I had to solemnly report to Ken that B.C. had an unfortunate sewing machine accident.

"Oh, NO", he said and looked around for her. Where was she? Did she get her paw in the way of the needle? Did she get sewn?

I tried hard to keep a straight face as I told him, no, she didn't get sewn, that WOULD have been a very unfortunate accident. What had happened had been almost as traumatic.

As usual, as I 'drove' the sewing machine by depressing the electric pedal, B.C. played innocently at my feet. Not thinking anything of it, I playfully moved my foot around, touching her belly, lightly stepping on her toes and quickly returning to my project. All of a sudden as I stopped my sewing, under my table B.C. started screeching with ear-piercing cat wailing. As I frantically looked down I could see that she had inserted her paw into the open pedal as I sewed; and, then as I stopped, the pedal had pinched her whole paw like a vise. In what must have been seconds (but what felt like eternity) I figured out what had happened and got down on the floor to open the pedal to release her paw from the trap. She was gone like a bolt of lightning. I was so sad, I had hurt my baby. Even if I didn't mean it, *I was very upset* with myself and feeling extremely guilty.

I called her but she stayed hidden under the bed, her pupils as big as marbles and every inch of her body trembling like a leaf in a violent wind storm. "Oh baby, Mama didn't mean it," I cried. She wasn't having any of it. Not long after, I found her in the hallway peeking out at me as if to ask "Is it safe to come out? What did *I* do, anyway?"

When she finally let me touch her I could see that her paw looked a little larger than the other and likely swollen, but by the time Ken arrived home, it was all just a funny story for dad. Soon both paws were back to normal size and so was B.C.'s natural cat curiosity.

Cat Chat

- *According to some reported studies, cats possess a surprisingly high intelligence and can remember problem solving strategies and use insight to figure their way out of difficult situations.*

- *Cat's paw: A light ripple on a calm sea, indicating the end of prevailing calm. Also a loop formed in a rope for attaching a hook.*

- *Cat's eye: A gem of changeable luster. Also a reflective glass stud embedded in roadway to aid motorists driving in the dark.*

- *Cat-call: Whistling noise people use to express displeasure.*

Proverb: Curiosity killed the cat. Satisfaction brought him back.

Chapter 14

—I Want My Yogurt!

We have, from the beginning, fed B.C. dry cat food only. I never could get myself to buy those little stinky cans of the moist stuff that gag you when you open them up. Ugh! And even though she is frequently curious when I am cooking in the kitchen, for the most part, I have resisted the temptation to 'give her just a bite'. Any time I have been tempted, Ken is quick to tell me not to do it. The last thing we wanted was a begging cat at the dinner table. That was one dog-like quality we did not want her to learn.

But somehow, as I drank my daily liquid yogurt the two of us started a sharing ritual. Early in the morning, she is just returning home from a long night of hunting and I am groggy from a Rumpelstiltskin-like slumber. One day I poured a quarter-size dollop of yogurt on a plate for B.C. to sample. She loved it and loudly pleaded in cat language what sounded to me like, "More please" for another taste. This became our morning routine.

B.C. would thank me by tickling my bare toes when I did not have slippers on with her emery board textured tongue which never failed to make me giggle.

Cat Chat

- Cats are lactose intolerant although some can eat small amounts of dairy products with no adverse affect. Room temperature water is best for cats.

- Cats prefer salty or bitter tastes. Cats do not crave sweets as they have no perception of simple sugars due to lacking a gene that detects sweet taste.

- A human has 9000 to 10,000 taste buds, a cat has only 473. A cat depends as much upon smell as taste on eating decisions.

- An internet search showed over 200,000 web sites available on subject of cat lovers.

Chapter 15

—Therapist in a Fur Coat

B.C. had been with us for two years when an unwelcome intruder showed up. It wasn't a skunk, although a skunk could be a mighty unwelcome visitor and I have always worried about her having a sad and smelly encounter with one. The uninvited and fearsome intruder's name was CANCER. At age forty-four, I was diagnosed with metastasized stage IV breast cancer. This was discovered following the removal of a hard, almond-size lump on my neck. Chemotherapy treatment would begin immediately and I was terrified beyond words or reason of what the future (or lack of a future) held for me.

B.C. and I pulled even closer during this time of turbulent storm in our lives. She had always needed me, but now I needed her just as much, too. No, I didn't need her to feed me or let me out of the house or change my litter as I did for her. But I needed her company and tranquil sound of soft purring that always comforted me.

I needed her to sit lovingly on my lap as I slept off the effects of chemotherapy. I needed her to make me smile with her playful antics. I needed the task of taking care of someone else. And she was always there for me. It is very mysterious how B.C. and I, different species, are seemingly able to connect and bond on such a deep emotional level.

Suddenly it was very apparent why the Universe had directed this sweet, silky angel to my doorstep two years prior. It was a test. You see, it has come to be my belief that in saving B.C. and making her part of our family that I earned the favor of having myself detained from a disease that, by all known facts, would take my life much sooner than I thought possible. But it hadn't yet, and I know that it is in good part because I had so many reasons to live. B.C. had responded to my love and attention when she first came to our house, barely alive and needing care and love. Now she would return the favor. Today, having been in remission from Stage IV breast cancer, but going through a second diagnosis, I am proud to say that I felt I had happily passed a test from this one life lesson.

Perhaps naming this small creature *Birthday Cat* was a wishful prediction that she and I would live to celebrate other birthday parties together. Or maybe it meant something more profound, such as why we cherish being alive enough to celebrate the occasion of our birth date and those of others on one special day each year we are alive. I began to think of every day as my birthday.

Cat Chat

- Both humans and cats have identical regions in the brain responsible for emotion according to some reported studies.

- People who own pets live longer, have less stress and have fewer heart attacks.

- Cats with calm temperament provide wonderful therapy for nursing home residents, particularly patients with Alzheimer's disease as they stimulate forgotten emotions and memories. Therapy cats should have necessary inoculations and trimmed or capped claws (using product such as SoftPaws™) for safety.

- The phrase, *to play cat and mouse*, refers to treating someone in your power as you like or teasing them unmercifully.

Chapter 16

—Still, Mama's Good Girl

Today, three years, nine months and eleven days from her 'delivery' date to our door, B.C. continues to be a source of fun, surprise, exasperation and love.

She is our little cat that acts like a dog. She is our baby, our daughter Lindsay's little 'sister' and our neighbors' friend (who according to Nathan Jones is *so soft* she makes him smile). She is our fierce hunter of the neighborhood, the ambush cat, our 'shredder in the office cat', a therapist in a fur coat, but mostly, "Mama's Good Girl." Cuddling with her always makes me feel warm inside and puts a smile on the outside. I love to smell the scents of dew, pine and wind on her fur when she comes in from outside. She is a welcome sight when we come home anytime. If I have been gone for longer than an afternoon, she will not let me out of her sight until she is convinced I am home for a good while.

B.C. is predictable most of the time and loveable all of the time. She is family. As I finish this story she sleeps soundly on our made bed dreaming, I believe, of how abundant her life has become . . . abundant in food, shelter and, best of all, love.

I have read somewhere that strays make the best pets. This has definitely been the case in our household.

It is my wish to all my readers that they, too, find the type of unconditional love that B.C. affords my husband and me. To us, she *IS* love.

A Wish for our Readers

Our wish for our readers is that by sharing our story, you will open your heart to the wonder of being a pet owner. If you are already so lucky, maybe you saw yourself and your beloved pet in some of B.C.'s story.

As in human relationships, choosing to share your home with a pet involves assuming certain responsibilities for the best results. The rewards are well worth the responsibility. They are rewards that can be considered priceless and include unconditional love, comic relief, and the comfort of companionship.

D.H. and B.C.

Afterword

—by Dolly Arksey

B.C.'s Letter (If a cat could talk)

A few weeks after my daughter Denise's death, it occurred to me one day as I watched B.C. tip toe and nose around the yard as if searching for something, or someone, that this kitty cat might be sadly missing the one special 'someone' she could always count on for extra attention. I thought it would be so interesting that if a cat could talk what would B.C. be saying right now? Immediately I began to imagine I could 'channel' B.C.'s thoughts. The words that flowed into to my mind are printed below in the form of a letter to Denise.

* * *

To Denise,

Where have you been? I keep waiting and watching for you every day, but it seems like such a long time since I have seen you. Did you forget me? My day does not seem complete without our morning yogurt shared treat or our mid-day nap with me on your lap in the big chair in front of the TV. I miss your gentle voice always reassuring me that you are happy to have me hang around.

If I could speak to you in your oddly garbled human sounds, I would tell you when I see you again how happy I am to have been adopted and invited into your life. Well, maybe if I just 'meow' with the right intonations, you will realize what I am trying to say. Luckily, that usually has worked okay in the past.

I know you love me by all you do to keep me safe. You will always be my best friend forever.

Miss and love you very much,

B.C.

The Birthday Cat will always have a special place in my heart, but before I explain more fully, I'd like to share some pre-B.C. history.

My first pet as a small girl was a stray, mutt dog with a raggedy black coat we named Pal. One day Pal just mysteriously appeared at our door and a couple of months later just as mysteriously disappeared. But while Pal 'lived' with us, I do remember how good it felt to have a furry friend to sit with me on the porch. I would put my arm around this scraggly, but wildly affectionate, dog and feel good about life and a lot less lonely. Pal was my first 'best friend'.

I have always been a 'dog person' for as long as I can remember. We have owned cats on and off briefly, but never developed a durable bond with any of the cats. Dogs have always seemed easier to deal with for my husband, Richard, and me. Maybe it was because dogs had the primary talent of being a built-in barking burglar alarm or door bell, which seemed like a job that warranted room, board and gratitude.

B.C., my daughter's exceptionally entertaining cat, seems different from cats I have known. As Denise put it, "This cat acts like a dog". I have not heard this cat bark yet, but would not be entirely surprised if it happened.

It was easy to recognize the very sensitive connection between my daughter and this golden-haired miniature lioness. This is especially so since their bond was forged under unusual circumstances as related in this book. B.C. also seems more affectionate than most cats I've known, even though she reserves plenty of 'aloofness' and privacy from strangers for herself as needed, for which she gets my full respect. We females know about stuff like that.

We can all take lessons from watching a cat. They have their daily routines down to simplified science:

1. eat
2. tend to personal hygiene
3. play
4. snuggle
5. nap
6. occasionally have a night "out on the town"

Repeat steps 1-5 above three or four times and you have the perfect day! Throw in step 6 to make life interesting.

A cat does not get itself into trouble by talking too much. A simple 'Meow' can describe several emotions—just change the volume and intonation. It helps to look directly at the person whose attention you are trying to get with wide imploring eyes. It is hard to make 'Meow' sound like an insult, so you are safe on that score. And purring is the best form of communication invented. I think a purring cat is saying, "Don't worry, be happy". Cats with personalities like B.C.'s are curious but cautious, sensitive but strong, and sociable but skeptical. This is definitely cat wisdom.

B.C. has charmed me into believing a cat is as good as a dog when it comes to bringing warm, fuzzy love, sophisticated companionship and entertainment into your life.

Cats have been 'personified' in cartoons and merchandise for our entertainment over the years including Felix the Cat, Garfield, The Pink Panther and the grinning Cheshire Cat in Alice in Wonderland. Andrew Lloyd Weber's, *Cats*, has been one of the longest-playing Broadway show successes. The book by Dr. Seuss, *The Cat in the Hat*, is a classic. The blockbuster movie and stage play, "The Lion King" story, will have super status as fictional feline tribute entertainment for many years to come.

The phrase "Cool Cat" is mid-to-late 20th century slang for someone who is, well, "Cool" before they changed it to "Hot".

Cats have captured our imagination throughout recorded history. Egyptians revered cats as evidenced in sculpture and ancient drawings. The lion and cat images are universal power symbols for many rulers and ancient civilizations and often depicted on temples and coat of arms insignias. Maybe this explains B.C.'s queenly mannerisms and high expectations of pampering.

All the large wild cats—lions, tigers, panthers, cougars, leopards and cheetahs—are feared and respected for strength and cunning. Domestic cats like B.C. have the same traits on a smaller scale to fit their diminutive size.

Cats in all shapes, sizes and temperament have played an important role in human history. It appears that they will continue to do so for the ages.

But the cat celebrity in our lives has been B.C., The Birthday Cat. The present she brought to the birthday party was herself and her performance arts. B.C. was the perfect gift at the perfect time for Denise because this tiny 'therapist in a fur coat' provided much comfort and diversion during periods of agonizing cancer treatments and unknown outcomes. This cat with the golden hair and golden eyes turned out to be a gift more precious than real gold.

B.C.—The Birthday Cat is a tribute to responsible cat ownership and a strong case for choosing a cat as a companion pet.

*   *   *

Afterward by Dolly Arksey, Denise Hammerberg's mother and co-author with Denise of The Garden of Being, non-fiction book (Booksurge 2007) and What Color Is A Bean?, illustrated children's book (Xlibris 2008).

* * *